THE CROSS OF CARL

THE CROSS OF CARL

AN ALLEGORY

The story of one who went down into
the depths and was buried; who, doubting
much, yet at the last lifted up his eyes
unto the hills and rose again and
was transfigured

By

WALTER OWEN

with a Preface by
GENERAL SIR IAN HAMILTON

Grey Suit Editions

This edition published in 2021 by
Grey Suit Editions, an affiliate
of Phoenix Publishing House Ltd.
First published by Grant Richards, Fronto Ltd, 1931

British Library Cataloguing in Publication Data
A CIP catalogue record for this book is available
from the British Library
Paperback ISBN: 978-1-903006-21-4
e-Book ISBN: 978-1-903006-22-1

Designed and set in Monotype Bulmer by Anvil

Printed and bound in the United Kingdom
by Hobbs the Printers Ltd

Frontispiece: Otto Dix, *Wounded Soldier (Autumn 1916, Bapaume)*: Tate Liverpool

Grey Suit Editions
33 Holcombe Road, London N17 9AS
https://greysuiteditions.co.uk/

CONTENTS

PREFACE

by General Sir Ian Hamilton

THERE IS something hypnotic in this stuff, something to cause the reader to fall into a state of hallucination! Until now never in my life have I come across anything quite like *The Cross of Carl*. Visions of Blake's mystical pictures; the passion, the exaltation, of Parsifal; the mystery, the unearthliness, of Coleridge; each in turn took possession of my mind as I read this strangest of all war stories. At other times the rhythm and style brought me back to De Quincey and once even to Jean Paul Richter: – "All the graves were unclosed, and the iron doors of the charnel-house were opened and shut by invisible hands. Shadows cast by no one flitted along the walls, and other shadows stalked erect in the free air." Yet not Richter nor Wagner nor Blake nor De Quincey can – though many of my friends will think it blasphemous to say so – hold a candle to this hapless, ill-starred wight named Carl. To me, and I dare only write as I think, Carl is more intense than the creations of those other great and famous men; dying, he is more there – more alive – even if he never was alive and never was really there! As to the Cross, was it a Victoria Cross made from the bronze of captured cannon; or was it not the "Eiserne Kreutz, Erste Klasse"; the Iron Cross; or, again, is the word symbolical, and may it not have been a fragment of the True Cross which Ann (or Anna?) found at the end when the seals were shattered and the crimson wax fell in flakes bedabbling dreadfully the floor?

God help us all!

Here is a book of ghouls, ghosts and nightmares in which Carl indeed shows up the whole tribe of those who write to make our flesh creep – the whole tribe from Edgar Allan Poe to Edgar Wallace – as so many amateurs. For even at the agony point of eerie happenings when an Emperor and his Field-Marshal emerge upon the desolate moor he never loses his grip upon the ground; not a slip does he make. One little nib-ful of ink is flicked on to paper and there stands the man of many parts and no part genuine, "his cloak aflap in the gentle wind that now stirred, his figure grey there in the whispering dawn." Another, gives us "a burly figure dressed in a Marshal's uniform ... His face was massive and heavy-jowled, a grim face with an eye to be feared –" and there stands the man who long ago, when something from "The Jungfrau von Orleans" was being quoted, exclaimed, "What is that I hear at my table? Poetry? Poetry!! In the heart of the Prussian Staff Officer there should be no room for anything but war!" Although Carl's adventure may become more and more fantastic, narrowing down fearfully into a grave, yet ever it continues to stick to the rails of reality; although never once has he looked upon either emperors or war with mortal eyes. How comes it, then, that he has been given power to make war more real to us soldiers even than the actual war? How has he been able to reproduce the very essence and spirit, the unhuman atmosphere of a mechanised modern battlefield?

A word of warning here. Only those armed with stout nerves and close-fitting gas masks should think of following Carl into the House from which blows a tainted wind, the sinister House which stands upon the moor of Golgotha. German women especially I would advise not to unlock the doors of that House: it holds horrors – horrors beside which Bluebeard's fabled chamber becomes a museum of sentimental keep-sakes.

By one of the coincidences of Fate the world is indebted for this unique revelation of the infernal regions to the notorious propagandist "Kadaver" lie. That same remarkable creative genius who made the foundations of a fortune out of fragments of other papers translated a captured German Corps order dealing with the removal of carrion into an order for the utilisation of human corpses. The carrion, i.e. the dead horses and sweepings of the slaughter-houses, was to be taken to a factory where it should be resolved into its elements of fat, manure, etc. The German for a human corpse is "Leiche"; for a dead animal "Kadaver." Here was a rare chance indeed. A mistake between "Kadaver" and "Leiche"; so simple; and the nation hitherto believed to be the most sentimental in Europe would then be represented as boiling up its fathers, sons, sweethearts, husbands, to squeeze out of them one last ounce of grease. Thus would millions of soldiers believe that the Fatherland was an Ogre, a monster devouring its own children, with whom it was impossible to come to terms. I doubt if even that master of propaganda imagined how far his joke would go or that it would make the devil break into the heartiest peal of laughter he has enjoyed since Cain killed Abel. For this masterpiece of hate has not only taken the shine out of the once notorious German Hymn of Hate, but is still pursuing its tortuous ramifications and has by now bred as many new hates as half a dozen pitched battles. Its intention was to make millions of men go on killing one another long after each fighting man felt he had suffered too much and had made the other men suffer enough. And no doubt it helped towards that end. But we see how Providence is working the Fat Factory now. Like a cloud of poison gas which is caught by an evil wind and blown back into the faces of the army which has launched it, so it has recoiled upon ourselves. All the water of the lake of Geneva won't quite wash out the foul "Kadaver" stain from the beautiful white peace and disarmament robes of those who too eagerly embraced that evil Thing.

Now it will live for ever though no longer to the detriment of the enemy: "The bodies come packed in bundles of four, naked, save for a rag of underclothing tied around their middles, and secured together by three ties of thick wire, tightly drawn, one in the middle and one at each end. At each end of the bale protrude two heads and two pairs of feet, the heads ghastly in their expressions of agony in all its moods, though now and then a face where peace has rested looks out and gives its blessing undismayed. The feet are pitiful: they that have come so far, and now must go this further, even when all their walks are taken."

Here is a living picture which will take as much killing as Carl. But who is Carl? I do not know. From me his identity is hidden. A man of business in the Argentine; that is all I have been told, and I do not even know whether he is British or German. Certainly the part of him which fought and died and was buried seems to have been German, else how could that naked man, "a tatter of rag still swathed about his hips . . . on his breast the red gash agape," answer the Marshal, saying, "Yes, I know you truly, you and the other there, but not as ye know yourselves, but in another glass than the eye scans." The Kaiser would have understood him; Hindenburg would not. But to attempt to measure phantasy with the foot rule of realism is waste of time. For myself, I am satisfied that whatever else or whoever else Carl may be he is genuine. An imaginative novelist would have written both worse and better. Very humbly I venture to submit that no writer now writing could have written some of the passages in this work. The professional craftsman would surely have worked out a bit of a plot and would have avoided the disorder and incoherence of certain passages. There is something to be explained which I at least cannot explain in the sudden appearance of a book from the Argentine by a man who, I believe, had never seen modern war with mortal eye and who yet manages to divest himself of all the paraphernalia and impedimenta of the old wars (which must have become more or less familiar to him in his youth) so as to visualise the attack on Hill 50 with a stark, concentrated realism which has been attempted, and yet not conveyed as he has conveyed it, by Tomlinson, Remarque, Barbusse and half a dozen other really first-flight authors. Consider these few lines taken from 'Gethsemane': "So at intervals picked snipers peered, here and there a periscope poked its inquiring nose, and the trench was like a queer beast that felt the air with horns. And Carl kept his nose low, like the rabbit that the good soldier knows so wholly how to be; while overhead death zipped and sang, and the rifle shots of the snipers pin-pricked here and there the thunder of the guns, like an impish tickle on a mammoth's flank or the puny staccato of crews of foundering barques over whom the ocean rolls. The guns were terrible that morning; dreadful like the voice of some Behemoth of man's making, whose works indeed when he strays from God are more terrible than God's, not greater, but grotesque and unholily deformed, dreadful as the abortions of an angel."

I appeal to those ex-Service men, several millions of whom can still recall the trench-sensation more easily than they can that of a lady's boudoir or a pub; men who have spent endless anxious hours gazing like so many lynxes through their periscopes at the enemy a few yards distant – I appeal to them and ask them whether anyone ever before brought back a trench to their memories as vividly as this Carl, or anywhere near so vitally? Next let them sample this inspired snippet from page 37 of the same chapter: "The air, too, was become the playground where in a carnival of passion immense presences danced with feet nimbler than the doe and wings swifter than swallow-wing. Their leap was whirlwind and the brush of their passing pinions vertigo unnamable." I would like to quote some of the battle reflections of Carl, especially on pages 42 and 43, but I must restrain myself lest the publisher should think I am trying to use poor Carl's book as the Utilisation Factory used his body and boil it down for copy as they boiled him up for fat. But I must just make this one further quotation for it goes beyond the book and brings us right back to the enigma of Carl's identity. See page 98 of the chapter 'Resurrection': "Then he" (Hindenburg) "stepped down with a heavy tread upon the body that lay there in the grave, and setting his foot upon the neck, pressed with a jerk of his full weight until the tautened sinews dragged the chin down to

dent the upper of his boot-toe. There was a dull snap."
At that fatal word "snap" the inspiration ceases. The
last two pages somehow – I cannot explain to myself
exactly how – seem to bring the whole of this terrible
edifice of the imagination tumbling on to the ground.
The burning Fat Factory that looked like a red eye over
the desolate moor; the shallow grave, a naked man
lying in it with a great wound in his breast: all this
vanishes in a twinkling of an eye like the Demon King
and his monsters in the Russian ballet of the Fire Bird
when the magic egg is shattered by the Prince. The
writing runs on; it is good writing; the style seems
the same. But it is writing not reality. And thereby
am I almost persuaded to believe that a phantasmal
projection from the mind or body of an Englishman
(or German) in the Argentine did go over the top and
actually attack Hell 50.

IAN HAMILTON

Kilbryde Castle
Dunblane
20th April, 1931

NOTE ON "THE CROSS OF CARL"

DURING the years 1916 and 1917 the writer was prevented from taking active part in the war by a physical affliction accompanied by severe pain which induced him to take quantities of opium as a sedative. In the first half of 1917 his mind became increasingly preoccupied with the moral and spiritual issues of the conflict. He suffered from attacks of melancholia which culminated in emotional crises. For some time these crises were confined to the chaotic nervous aberrations classified as hysteria by neurologists. But towards the end of the month of June 1917 he observed that the termination of the nervous paroxysm marked the commencement of a third phase. The general characteristics of this third phase were in complete opposition to those of the preceding condition. There was a great sense of well-being, of peace, poise and power. The mind was exceptionally lucid and alert. Physical discomfort and disabilities were non-existent. Spiritually there was a feeling of integration, dispassion and purposiveness.

So marked and peculiar was this condition that he made notes, from which he compiled the following table of observations.

PHYSICAL:

Partial analgesia, not localised, i.e. sensibility diminished, *in degree,* to pain, cold, hunger, fatigue and bodily weakness.

Hyperæsthesia specifically localised in the sensations of sound, light and touch. Motor automatism of varying intensity (automatic and semi-automatic script). Pulse 10 to 20 above normal (100 average). Breathing very slow (3 to 4 per minute). Temperature above normal (99°).

MENTAL:

Rapid and clear perception of phenomena.

Supernormal lucidity, alertness and coordination.

Effortless recollection of all past impressions.

Expansion of sense of space and time.

Imaginative luxuriance.

Exceptional power of rhythmical and musical speech.

Impairment of the power of verbal visualisation (bad spelling).

PSYCHIC:

Obliteration of the psychic diaphragm normally existing between the conscious and subconscious elements of personality. Extinction of the passional and egocentric emotions such as fear, anger, aversion, hatred, acquisitiveness.

Voluntary heteraesthesia, i.e. the power of projecting the sensibility into any selected object, whether organic or inorganic, conscious or unconscious.

Occasional polylocationary consciousness (involuntary); by this is meant the sensation of being in two or more places at the same time.

Visual and auditive automatisms manifesting as flashes of pale blue light of great intensity; and a sound of singing voices accompanied by music.

A sense of spiritual completeness and exaltation.

Whether the abnormal condition described was induced by the administration of opium or whether the opium was merely a contributory factor, the writer is unable to say. About the middle of the month of July 1917 he suffered a particularly severe attack of depression which was relieved by the usual nervous paroxysm, but, this time, of exceptional violence, which gradually subsided into the third phase. At the commencement of the third phase on this occasion he experienced a vivid bilocation of consciousness. So clear and complete was his sensation of being in two places at once that his entire personality appeared to be double. One of these personalities was his customary one, with the modifications tabulated above. The other was that of a soldier in the trenches of one of the battlefields, who was about to take part in a dawn-attack. A circumstance which he observed particularly was that, making allowance for the difference in locality, the hour in both places synchronised perfectly. The secondary personality was in no sense a mental marionette of his own, but an individual with whose name, history, relatives, social ties and mental and spiritual make-up he was as familiar as with his own. At the same moment that he experienced this bilocation of consciousness he was prompted to record in writing the experiences of this soldier. It is this record, without alteration except for the condensation of certain portions of the chapter entitled 'Golgotha' (which seemed to him of too revolting detail), that forms the narrative of *The Cross of Carl*. During the writing of it he was a spectator of, and actor in, the events related; and he underwent the experiences of his "alter-ego" even more vividly than if they had been actually objective, as a consequence of the heightened sensitiveness and lucidity which accompanied his condition of dual consciousness. The partial analgesia mitigated, but did not render him entirely immune from, the physical suffering inherent in Carl's experiences. As it was, there was repercussion from the body – real or illusory – of Carl to his own body, to the extent that he felt the external physical impact of the wounds described, and that a superficial stigmatisation appeared at the seat of the injuries and endured for a few hours. He also while writing suffered occasionally from nervous collapse and underwent in a milder degree the other sensations described, with the exception of the attack of nausea which was violent and prolonged.

The foregoing will explain why the writer disclaims for *The Cross of Carl* any pretension to form a narrative of actual objective experience in the customary sense of the words. He believes, however, that he is warranted in putting it forward as an authentic personal record of an abnormal pathological process induced by the psychic perturbations which formed the background of the physical conflict. He is not prepared to assert that the impressions received by him through his bilocated consciousness have any other validity. They may have been objectively veridical; they may have been hallucinatory; or they may have been impressions received from some extraneous source and which possess a purely symbolic significance. The immediate recipient of those impressions may have been a material frame inhabited by a separate consciousness between which and his own a rapport was established of such immediacy as to constitute a temporary fusion of personalities. It may have been a phantasmal vehicle disengaged from his own physical body and utilised in an actual psychical excursion. Or, again, it may have been a vision originating in his own mind. Upon such matters he has formed no judgment. But there is no doubt in his mind that there are subtler and more potent forces in operation in the world than those externalised to the senses, and that during the late war the spiritual and mental atmosphere of humanity underwent far-reaching modifications as the result of a period of agitation manifesting the essential symptoms of a neurotic paroxysm. His own particular temperament, conditioned by his hypersensitised condition, probably rendered him specially susceptible to those forces and induced in him a temporary functional activity of faculties latent in the normal consciousness. It is to his mind suggestive that in his case the neurotic explosion was superseded, albeit temporarily, by a

24

third phase in which the higher faculties of the ego appeared to be liberated and expanded; and it may not be beyond the bounds of probability that that third phase may be in some degree the foreshadowing of a development in the collective consciousness of mankind of which the first indications are gradually becoming apparent at the present time.

Everything in this story is purely symbolical

CONTENTS

"Though I walk through the valley of the shadow of death, I will fear no evil, for Thou art with me, Thy rod and Thy staff they comfort me."

Psalm XXIII. 5

These waters were not poured except to heal and wash; nor was the vessel troubled save with love and pity towards all men, which being of the vessel earthly, in measure clouded them with blood and tears.

I
GETHSEMANE

CARL SHIFTED his weight from one foot to the other on the fire-step and leant his body as much as possible against the front wall of the trench. Usually such relief was not to be had, for Carl was sturdy and inclined to fat, but here the rain, which for the last three days had ceaselessly poured, had carved a little gully that ran from the parapet to the step, so that Carl lay half cradled in the embrace of the earth, and his legs, which since he left his home a week ago had gradually grown wearier, till they were a permanent ache to him, found thus, for a space, relief from a portion of his weight.

His rifle lay across the parapet in front of him, bayonet fixed, but Carl's eyes did not rove foeward, for that way here the unwary soul departs quickly, and the red spout of blood in a trench that waits the signal for a dawn attack is not beloved even by the best-tempered lieutenant.

So at intervals picked snipers peered, here and there a periscope poked its inquiring nose, and the trench was like a queer beast that felt the air with horns. And Carl kept his nose low, like the rabbit that the good soldier knows so wholly how to be; while overhead death zipped and sang, and the rifle-shots of the snipers pin-pricked here and there the thunder of the guns, like an impish tickle on a mammoth's flank or the puny staccato of crews of foundering barques over whom the ocean rolls.

The guns were terrible that morning, dreadful like the voice of some Behemoth of man's making, whose works indeed when he strays from God are more terrible than God's, not greater, but grotesque and un-holily deformed, dreadful as the abortions of an angel. And truly the ground on which Carl lay was like some beast that heaved in birth-pang, in the throes of a pain too big, too big for earth, and the air shuddered with the breath of its woe. Now it grumbled like Vulcan, far off in bowels of adamant and granite, and then a gust took it and it shook afresh, gathering its blast; and the scale of its breath was the gamut of madness, and the anthem that it sang, the anthem of the agony of all the choir of hell that sang to the baton of Abaddon the Trisagion of Pandemonium – unholy! unholy! unholy! Sometimes a lull made an island in the roar, but when it burst again, only more terribly did its billows roar, and more brutal the bellow with which it shook the blue.

At such times Carl clutched the ground with trilling tympanums and bastinadoed brain, conscious dully of the grey clay an inch beyond the goggles of his gas mask. Silly things kept coming into his head. He wondered what they would be having at home for breakfast. He tried to think of his wife, but found that he could think of nothing except the breakfast. This was perhaps because he was hungry. Then a terrific burst of sound swept over him, and suddenly he recalled what he had heard a girl say to her lover at the station the day he entrained. She had said: "Remember to be careful." It seemed so unutterably silly! Careful! That was woman all over. She should be here, the silly!

Then he remembered his wife, and how he had told her that he would bring her back the cross. His mind went back to the time when he was not fat, when he had wooed her in the long twilights after work; of their walks along roads deepening in the dusk, and the marriage in the village church – just a little hurried, perhaps, for they were human, these two – and of their first child. He put up his hand to wipe some mist from his goggles, but the mist was not there on the outer glass. . . . Over Carl, too, those wings had hovered.

He turned at a slap on the leg and saw the sergeant passing along the trench. The man on his right put his nozzle, grotesquely like the muzzle of a dog, close to his ear and yelled through to him: "We go over at eight, Fatty. It's five to, now. When you see the signal, over you go. We've got to get Hill 50." "Where's Hill 50?" Carl called back at him. The man waved his arm. "Straight ahead," he said. "But it's all the same; you'll never get there. It might as well be Hell 50."

Inside his stuffy mask Carl darkled. The man's words waked in him a strange rage. What was he here for? What were they all fighting about, these fools, with their Hill 50, which might be Hell 50, and which was to be got to, but could not be got to by the fruit of woman? If they would only stop that infernal racket! The cross? What had the cross to do with this place of fifty hells, of tabulated infernos? Wrath swept through him – and his poor flesh, empty now for many an hour, trembled in its hollow. He raised his hands and beat the clay before his face. "Curse the cross!" he shrieked into the unheeding womb of din. "Curse the cross! – curse the cross!"

So said Carl in his ditch that dim morning, while the Beast that man had made raged round him and wound him ever further and firmer in its toils. And you

34

were right, Carl, as man is in the main right and men in the mass are in the main wrong; but you should have stopped at that last, Carl, for that was a hard thing to say, now; and out there Death reaps with a free sweep and singing scythe; and not with curses in his heart is it fit that a man should meet his Maker.

*   *   *   *   *   *

The signal had been given, and Carl, scrambling upward on hands and knees, had sprawled across the wet clay of the parapet, risen grasping his rifle, and now was off at a shambling run over ground sodden with rain and dotted with shell-pools. He ran awkwardly, as the middle-aged man runs on whose thews the fat has set old encroachment; and the mud squelched and slithered under the blunder of his big boots. Enveloping him, a shroud of mist and smoke drove and whirled and drifted; and in front a curtain hung, behind which the concussions of the barrage gambolled redly, throating always its oratorio.

Little as had been his idea of the plan of attack and the part set apart for his battalion, it was now no better; only he knew that he was one of a crowd that straggled out across the open, death-dedicated, their faces set towards a bourne unknown. Dreadful to him seemed their ineffectual pace and grotesque the spludge with which they trudged the mud. Could sacrifice be so shorn of outward grandeur, could things ultimate enough to fling millions at each other's throats be served by figures so ineffectual and ridiculous? Not so, surely, did Gaul and Ossian lean forward into battle, nor Hector leap the Grecian ditch. True, Carl, true – but in the end the last chapter of the body's story is the same; one sure touch deep-biting on head or breast or belly, and the red honey that the soul stored pours, and she, the bee, is gone. Look, now.

On the edge of a crater he saw a man in front kneel down as though to pray there, at which Carl, this being his first charge, and indeed his first taste of war at all, hurried to him, and was just about to touch him when the man went forward on his face limply in the clay, and at the same instant another figure some three yards on his right said "Ah!" and, gasping, sprawled.

At this Carl stood a space dazed, not knowing what to do, his throat choking and his heart aflutter; then going to the first man, he put down his hand and touched him, saying in a sort of whisper "What is it?" and, without waiting to know, was off a few steps to the other, and over him, too, he leaned, and peered, and said again "What is it?" in a sort of whisper. But scarcely had he spoken when he was answered; for the man rolled over in his death agony, and as he gasped, the death-rattle blew from his torn throat in a splutter of red over Carl's bent be-goggled muzzle.

At that Carl started back, and had just time to see a leg severed at the hip lying bloody-stumped apart from that other huddle on the crater's edge, when he heard dimly a shout behind, and looking, saw the sergeant with revolver pointed at him coming up through the haze. He could hear nothing of the words flung at him but understood the menacing murder of that glance and that glinting barrel, and terror urged him forward.

He turned and plunged into the mist ahead, plugging the mud heavily, his rifle trailing, and a weakness in his knees, for death is not pretty, and he had not seen it near before. In front he saw the backs of his fellows jogging slowly forward, all moving one way, in twos and threes; here and there a single figure, and at intervals larger patches, where many shadows blurred to one mass.

Suddenly he found himself in a crowd. He saw two officers close to him. One seemed to be urging the men forward, the other hung upon the rear, moving this way and that, as a collie cuddles the rear of his flock. In his hand was an automatic. At that Carl spurted anew, and drew up into the middle of the crowd.

As yet he had seen no man, other than those first two, fall. He wondered if, after all, it might be that by taking care one might win a trick from death. Assuredly that was it. Those two back there had not: been careful. Perhaps even Hill 50 might be hell only for its defenders. He brought his rifle from the ground – and a tall man beside him turned, threw up his arms and clutched him with a squeal, his mask a red mash.

They went down together, the tall man atop, drumming frantically with his toes, his head pressed tight against the breast of Carl's tunic. Carl struggled free, and rose. The officer in front was gesticulating. With one hand he pointed at the mist ahead, and with the other he seemed to gather the air behind him, and fling it forward. There was a rush around him, a chug-chug of many feet. He ran with the others.

The smoke opened and ahead he saw a mound against a further murk, the remains of what once had been a hill, now a monstrous tumble of rubbish, like the midden of a Cyclops or a birth begotten of earthquake. From a dozen points smoke poured from it, and he caught a glint just under the ragged rim of its ridge. Then Hill 50 spoke, and justified the jest upon its name.

Three horizontal bands, one above the other, crashed into flame upon the crouched hunch of the mound, and as the air knew that jar it shuddered and its riven chambers crashed heart-shatteringly. Cataract after cataract of sound poured; Niagaras of thunder gambolled amid a din of tumbling Gibraltars; and over their jostling battlements the trumps of judgment brayed their blast of desolation. The sun was a brass that banged and the earth answered with her voice in travail.

The air, too, was become the playground where in a carnival of passion immense presences danced with feet nimbler than the doe and wings swifter than swallow-wing. Their leap was whirlwind and the brush of their passing pinions vertigo unnamable. Here and there they whooped and stooped and flew, bruising the poor earth, burrowing to burst there deep their fiery hearts and throw fields skyward in steel-shot fountains. Overhead, while the eye pondered its flutter, their sirocco grew to full, and ere the lid drooped they whooped their whaup and went.

Before that onslaught Carl's band went down like penned cattle above which the red sledge is busy. Three level sheets of flame fraying out from the hill's three bands of fire, converging, took them on a single edge of steel, solid almost as an axe-blade. The first ranks, cut in two by that dreadful stream of death, wilted and were no more, and the blade, passing on, bit ever deeper into the huddle of the ranks behind. A blanket of burning air swept down on Carl, filling his lungs through the mask he wore. A jumble of screams beat in to him from in front, and above the heads before him he saw a toss of arms and a shattered rifle spin.

Then the man upon whose heels he trod burst like a puff-ball. He seemed to blow out and go, burst into a whirl of shattered bone and flying blobber, and where he had been his cut-off shriek hung. Carl's mask was torn from his face, the left ear-strap taking with it half the ear, and now Carl, too, conscious of that cruel pang, screamed. Something hit his bare face, something warm that squelched and fell at his feet, leaving his eyelids heavy. Dazed, as one does such things, he stooped, saw it red and twitching under his hand and screamed again. Then he turned and, with the goad of that horror deep in his soul, leapt into the mist whence he had come.

But now no more does he know where to go, nor how to guide his heavy feet. The air is an inferno of flying fragments, dust and flame; everywhere those murderous devils leap, and where they strike chaos thuds to being, and being in her turn to chaos. And, through all, the screaming sears, a high-pitched continuous ululation like the lamentation of damned souls.

He takes a step, and before him hell opens a new mouth; his next leap is sideways, and a gaunt corpse, from which the uniform streams in crimson tatters, whirls spread-eagled at him, swooping like a great strange bird from a cloud of smoke. He avoids its flight, and is off like a harried rabbit at an angle when his foot twirls in a hole and he is down. As he rises a man, or what has been a man, comes down on top of him and crushes him in the mud. A weight presses his chest, and through his tunic a warm moisture soaks his skin. . . .

Again he struggles up, pushing that nameless thing from him, his mouth a-twist; and, when once more he stands, his tunic from collar to waist is no longer grey but red. Down his neck his torn ear, too, pours its quota, his helmet hangs backward, the tatters of his gas-mask are twisted about his throat. Around him, as far as he can see on either side beneath the pall of vapour, to front and rear, the plain is like a pot of mud that has been stirred, and in which great bubbles, bursting, have left their pits. And over all that tumbled plain lies the harvest that the guns have gathered, the crops of flesh that are man's toll to the Beast that he has made.

Here like a sheaf three bodies stand leaned together, planted to the knees in mud, one headless, one with a jagged fragment of steel projecting from its back, the other unmarked save for a trickle at the lips. Near these a carcase, without legs or arms and caked with clay, lies like a grey valise. Further is a leg naked and blackened; a boot protrudes, a rifle with a hand and forearm hanging from it sticks butt upward. There is a huddle of bodies in one place piled one upon the other, and away from that heap something drags itself upon its hands, something like a maimed dog that lifts a blackened head and howls. . . .

Hill 50 has spat her spit for this time, but her chosen children, the snipers, cuddle their rifle-butts in her ditches yonder and peer steady-eyed into the mist. And at the moving thing they see they aim, and where they aim they hit. As Carl stands a bullet rips the flesh of his shoulder. He is hurt, but not to death; a numbness runs down his arm, and again that warm flow that he knows spreads under his clothes.

But the touch of the foe's bullet wakes him from the daze of that first battle-terror that all warriors know. Fear passes from him. He sinks, crawls behind the body lying there and rests his rifle across it. There is a glint on the hill and Carl's first bullet wings. His is a kill.

A dozen empty cartridge-cases lie in the shelter of his bulwark, when he is conscious of a confused noise behind. It grows and disintegrates into the chug-chug of many feet that plough the mud. It is the attack, re-formed and reinforced, coming back upon its dreadful tracks to batter at Hill 50's gates.

Far to the right and left behind him he sees the forefront of the attackers breaking through the mist, and beyond that fringe the mass of the wave looms hugely through the fume. Abruptly the dribble of shots from Hill 50 stops, and it, too, looms, glowering and still, like a crouched monster at bay that shakes the slaver from its chin and braces itself to meet the on-slaught of the hounds. Between, time tenses and the air holds its breath.

The first man shuffles past Carl some twenty yards to his right, then three together pass close to him. As Carl rises one of them brings his rifle half-way to the shoulder, but, at Carl's shout, drops it, waves his hand forward and is off. Carl now brings his rifle to the carry and, after the man, he too goes, plugging the mud.

He feels no pain now, nor again can panic take him, but he goes deliberate and wrathful. It is as though there are in him two Carls, one above, calm, resolute, unshaken, and an under-Carl which is a creature of passion and hot anger and red frenzy, like an elemental born from the torture of a slaughterhouse. And the upper-Carl, which is master, stoic and Spartan, callous as pure reason and pitiless as arithmetic and Euclid, observes, directs and prompts the Carl its creature, whispering, "Carl, do this," or "Carl, go there," or "Quick, Carl," and that under-Carl obeys.

For thus does battle divide man within himself – against himself, since the body, as the state, in which such rule is, though it endure a little, passes; yet again for himself in the end and long-run of the æons, since from the unconscious oneness first must come division before the conscious wedding that is peace.

And man is then as it were god and devil – god in the austere far-seeing plan, and devil in that blind and brutal hacking that the mandate launches; yet false god and false devil, since not these either may endure in the end and long-run of the aeons, any more than the God of pure man-righteousness and the Devil of pure man-sin that man's heart has set in his mind's temple; but must ultimately meet, they too, and mate and have their bridal sweets.

And man, although as yet but half awake and still slumber-eyed, dimly even now perceives this; and in that temple a whisper stirs that the priests cannot wholly keep from the ears of their sheep. . . . "For God without the devil cannot be human, now, nor our Father surely; and your Devil, too, he must be God, not to be divorced from Him – yea, Him vehemently by pitiless Euclid and urgently by arithmetic, since the Whole must contain the part, and He is all that is. . . ."

And now that atom that is Carl runs there at Hill 50, doing his bit in the long wooing; and the Hill glowers at him over the gloom, biding its time for the bit that is its to do. . . .

He has fallen back somewhat, for he limps, his ankle swollen so that he has had to cut open his right boot, and he is in the midmost of the wave of those grey figures that move forward like beaters shooing unseen game.

No man falls as yet, no yelp or growl sounds from hounds or quarry. The foremost men come to the remnants of smashed and tangled wire and posts splintered and askew on which a few dark bundles of rags hang sagging woefully, like scarecrows propped amid the crops of murder. They pick their way through the mass, and now, at that tangled barrier's nearer edge, little crowds begin to gather, waiting to pass, for parts are impassable and the fords narrow.

In a moment the crowd grows, and those behind still come on, men with teeth set and lips a-twitch. An officer yells and flings up his hand in front there. A man beside Carl turns to him: "The fools!" he shouts, "the fools! – They should have seen if it was clear. Look at them. It's murder!" He flings himself into a shell-pit, Carl beside him. A confused noise comes from ahead. He can see a man in front, facing round, beat the air downwards with his palms as a conductor stills an orchestra. Hill 50 opens.

For the second time Carl feels that tornado batter at his brain and his sanity swims – the giggle and tee-hee of madness not far from his lips then – but the upper-Carl, with a wrench, masters and, as those thunders leap about him and discharge their wrath heart-shatteringly, croons bemused above his racking flesh, murmuring "This one" – and, as it passes, "No, the next" – and again, "This one" – and as that, too, goes whooping its whaup, he looks upward to its uproar and grins, wagging his hand in a gleeful ta-ta. Then he raises his head above the shelter of the shell-hole's rim and looks, and the next moment is out and running to the wire.

The attack this time has wilted but not broken, for it is deep, and where one wave halts and tumbles its grey froth, another, roaring in, tumbles its grey froth in turn further, throwing out, as it frays, streams that reach out like feelers ever nearer to the Hill. The solid foam of bodies leaves a ridge where the wire stretched its tangle, and, behind that slight shelter, the billows of the charge gather, then, mounting, pass ceaselessly to break and seethe and cease. Ranks are cut as by scythe-blades, invisible flails leap laughing here and there, monstrous devils of iron, soaring slowly, swoop through the smoke and, bursting, smash islands in the tight-packed crowd, throwing up eruptions of earth and shattered flesh. But ever the grey waves mount and spread and the grey froth rolls nearer, nearer, yearning shorewards to the Hill. . . .

From all that mass of shattered man a myriad screams and moans that the ear weaves weakly to one fabric rise like a steam of pain. Something else, too, rises, intangible and supersensual, but hypnotic, soul-compelling, too rare for eye's dark glass or ear's dull drum to gather, airy as a babe's dream, yet stark as a crown of thorns biting at the brow – as it were the brush of wings innumerable, woven to a presence tender and terrible at once, that rises sheathed in splendours and crowned with sacrifice above the agonies of earth. The herd in their bloody quagmire feel it move

47

among them as a wave and, for a space in that choked communing-place of life and death, where the carnate and the discarnate mingle, the iron bands of the body and its terrors drop, and the carnate act as the discarnate, are lifted, masters, above themselves, become gods and devils, know themselves immortal and divine. . . . Pain sends up to them no message, weariness drops like a husk, death – there is no Death. . . .

The packed mass slides forward roaring, mounts in front there, thrusting forward its breast thirstily upon that edge of reaping steel, indomitable, not to be denied its Hill. It is horrible, it is dreadful, but it is sacramental. . . . Look down, O God! – here in the shambles man vindicates again his claim and the faith by which he lives; here, as in a figure of things spiritual, Adam turns again to the guardian of the Garden, his breast against that flaming blade, and in his mouth the shout: "Make way! . . . Thou canst slay, but not destroy!"

The attackers now reach to fifty metres from the first trench upon the Hill. A minute passes, and the gap is twenty metres. A new spout of flame roars from the Hill's volcano and the gap widens to thirty, then closes with a rush to ten.

Carl is now mounting the ridge where the wire was, packed tight among a hustle of figures that bear him onward in their rush. He is treading on bodies on which his feet slip and blunder. It is like walking on bolsters full of stones. Bones pop underfoot. He looks down and sees a face give under his boot, then slides and comes down. A gnashing mouth closes on his leg; he frees himself and is up again. A lane crashes through the crowd, missing him narrowly, and a welter of fragments whirls round him. A man in front goes down on his knees and, shrieking, grabbles blindly at a stringy mass that pours downward from the lower part of his body, trying madly to mend that cruel hurt that is past all mending. Carl leaps over the man and goes on. He is nearing that dreadful edge where the crowd frays into a fringe of death. Hill 50, slavering at him with flaming breath, looms above.

The first of those three trenches is now not more than ten metres in front. He finds suddenly only one man in front covering him, and they run together with a spurt. Two metres they cover thus – three. The trench is five metres off, when the man goes down, and Carl, springing over his body, drives on, his bayonet forward, all the lump of him lumbering ponderously, his knees now at last feeling again their weariness, but the upper-Carl still master, the lower still obeying.

A face in a helmet appears at the level of the ground, a hand-grenade whizzes past his head. Here are Hill 50's children. He lunges forward at the head, and the bayonet, entering at an eye, bites with a rasp upon bone, and sticks fast. At the same instant he receives the thrust of a bayonet in turn. Aimed at his belly, it is a fraction too high; the steel grates on the sternum and rips upwards its pitiless gash till, deflected by his left hand that now leaves his own rifle to seize that other, it sticks under his right clavicle, but owing to its direction from below upward, does not enter far, although it lacerates the top of the lung. Also a bullet goes through the flesh of his left calf, touching the bone, but not breaking it.

But Carl, though pain stabs dully, shifts the grip on his rifle, gets the trigger and pulls, at which the impaled head drops away from the bayonet. He now has the other's rifle firmly held in his left, and, though the man pulls, Carl is no weakling, and his weight is firmly anchored.

Suddenly the other man lets go the rifle, and, as he grabs a hand-grenade, Carl's bullet brings him night. Carl stumbles into the battered trench, and as he crumples on its floor sees all along the wave of the attack sweeping in and a tumble of leaping figures and clubs that rise and fall. There is no surrender. Hill 50, too, has her vision and her faith, and her firm-lipped children that fight like devils die like gods.

But Carl is in a bad way now. Things are slipping from him. He feels the trench swing like a ship beneath him and as in a dream hears a voice murmur at his ear. With the palsy of swoon creeping on him he puts his hand to the wound in his breast and, sipping deliciously the poppy-boon of sleep, his tired mind sinks into the plush of dreams. . . .

Far back, on the other side of Hill 50, an officer in a dim dug-out, with a telephone clipped to his head, reaches out his hand to a button and presses it. The set of mines had been well laid as a counter for the possible loss of that first line, a backward gnash of the hill as she withdraws a little and hunches herself further in her ambush . . . and that gnash now crunches.

Five mine-chambers set deep at intervals of a hundred yards, each well gorged with deadly food, with cunningly knuckled tunnelling to absorb the backblast and heavy tampions of cement and sand-bags, burst upwards as with one shock beneath the battered trench, their voices blending in one terrible roulade at which the Hill rocks, and five separate mushrooms of soil sprout monstrously and spread and burst, throwing far and wide fountains of debris, battered guns, riven cement blocks, beams and wire, rifles, smashed ammunition boxes and remains of men.

* * * * * *

Late that day, in a far-off town, in the garret that she had crept to with her children, Ann, the wife of Carl, sat at the tiny window through which the gloaming darkled, a boding in her heart not to be banished, for she had had no word from him since he went, though he had promised; and she remembered that at that promise she had winced in her woman's wisdom, knowing, as all women know, that for every man's promise a bow is strung whose shaft will some day wound a woman's heart. And when the postman came his round she raised her head eagerly yet feared to go to the door; and, when she heard his footfall fade and die, suddenly she bowed her brows there on her arms upon the table, and her shoulders shook; for all her woman's home was reft of its man that night, and the hearth of her heart cheerless, like the cabin where the fisher's wife waits lonely with her light and sadly watches, knowing only that her Jo is on the ocean, but where, in all its desolation and tramp of billows, she knows not. ... And in the gathering shadows, presently, she slept.

But Carl lay that night on Aceldama; and a gentle rain fell upon his upturned face, and upon all who lay there with him, God as it were sweating in His heaven with pity, while below man groaned in the Gethsemane of his flesh; and his sweat was blood.

But Carl was not dead; for him wait deeper depths than these, aye, and greater heights. His grave is not yet dug, and in three days he must dig it with his hands.

II

GOLGOTHA

O NE HUNDRED miles from Hill 50, as the kite flies up a tainted wind, a group of buildings stands upon a moor. Between it and the Hill stretches a rolling country, dotted here and there with villages, mottled with a dark rash of forests and wealed lividly with rivers that gurgle slowly to the sea.

It is a dark land and desolate, for over the larger part of it war's juggernaut has crashed and, though many months have passed since that time of terror, man has been too busy feeding its wheels yonder where it has stuck in its ruts, to trouble overmuch to mend the scars and tramplings of its track. In the villages grass grows its green beard around the cobbles, save in those through whose shuddering streets food is dragged daily to the Beast. Forests have been felled in acres to make room for road and railway; groups of ruins stand gaping gloomily amid lopped and riven trees. People are scarce save in the arteries that yield that ceaseless tribute whose drain the land now begins sorely to feel.

Through the forests, wild winds, for it is winter, throat their low note of moaning. Sometimes church bells toll, but weakly and appealingly, a wail which the people hear indeed but heed no more than the elfin bells that sleepy shepherds hear along the evening hills, though sometimes they go in and move their lips dully in that House that might be Rimmon's house to them. For the priests have mostly been smitten dumb by the blast of Baal's passing and the voices of those that still speak are a sound in which small comfort is. But the soul knows, as indeed she knows all, that by that road, though on it night gathers, dawn comes; and wearily still the mind plods to her urge, though no star beams now. And the flame burns always, though deep, and the earth, knowing, makes her attack to smother; but, though not yet is the fire's victory, the day comes when the clay shall be riven and the sky kindled with the fire's begotten. . . .

Southward on the moor the land rolls flatly and bare, save for low bushes for many a mile; northward, some two miles from the group of buildings, a river sweeps in a curve, and on the other side is a small town, north of which again the land goes more pleasantly, fruitful with the crops whereby man's body lives. Eastward, far away, a low range of hills tumble the horizon lazily.

Over these hills at dawn the sun views the moor always sullenly, for every night a night-sweat falls there, no sweet dew, but the clammy moisture of marshes, such as in great part the moor is; and, like an evil thing that has settled to a work unholy, this, at the first hint of day, rises in a thick vapour through which the sun, when he comes, glares redly.

The buildings stand far out on the moor. There are three main structures, a central large one, oblong, about fifty yards long by twenty wide, and, on either side of this, narrower sheds of almost equal length, evidently accessory to the main buildings, like covered platforms for loading and discharging. A cluster of out-houses completes the group, all hideously constructed of galvanised sheeting and raw girders, liberally daubed with whitewash.

Round all a light railway runs, with sidings to the two platforms, a gimcrack, uneven way with small pretence at ballasting even on that bad soil, as if its maker, too, felt guilty, and the sun, peering over the hill some morning, might find him gone with all his traps. The buildings are completely circled by a double fence of barbed wire, eight feet high, curved inwards at the top. Inside this an inner fence, a few wires high, edges the railway line.

Along the edge of the wood to the westward runs a road, cut at a level-crossing by the railroad, which disappears into the wood there.

At six every morning there is a bustle among the hutches out yonder. Men come and go between the shed and the platforms. The railway creaks and rattles under the rumble of closed trucks; an engine puffs. From a chimney in the main shed smoke pours and in the air an acrid odour spreads.

At five in the afternoon the noises and the smoke cease. Gradually the figures that now move again round the hutches grow fewer, a light gleams for a little hour or two like an eye watching, and then another night shuts down and the mist settles.

Only one or two men pass and return through the single gate in the fence, where constantly a sentry watches in a box. Through this gate, which is a heavy iron frame, backed by wire-netting and surmounted by barbed wire, the single track of the railway passes, the gate being just wide enough to admit a truck. It is secured by a massive, old-fashioned lock, the key of which hangs in the sentry's box.

The men who pass in and out are three; always the same three, each taking a salute from the sentry as he goes, and going silently with grim looks. No others of the workers ever go out, but live in the hutches yonder. The only others who have passage to and from the world outside the high barbed fence are the guard and driver of the train that puffs fussily through the gate in the daytime; and they are always the same men.

Over all this place a silence broods, heavy as the stillness of sodden grass through which the wind's feet no longer stir, with something malignant and guilty mixed into its stillness, as if the grass concealed a corpse. A nameless suspicion filters to the soul through the eye that looks upon it, and a fear such as the traveller feels when on the heath at night he passes a pool, fringed with long grass, from which the moon's floating pupil watches.

A mesmeric influence seems to draw the gaze that surveys the moor to those buildings that show white against its dark face, like a tumble of bleached bones over which a savour of decay still hangs. The soul says that this is an evil place, though the mind may scoff; and the soul, as always when she speaks, is right.

These buildings are the Utilisation Factory of the Tenth Army Section and to them the bodies of the slain in battle are dragged over that ramshackle railroad, sometimes almost before the blood's warmth is quite chilled, and while some grosser streamers from the departing guest still linger in the brain's grey maze, hearing dully the summons from without.

The bodies arrive in covered trucks drawn by a fussy engine, with pantings and shrieks that seem deliberately devilish. The bodies come packed in bundles of four, naked, save for a rag of underclothing tied around their middles, and secured together by three ties of thick wire, tightly drawn, one in the middle and one at each end. At each end of the bale protrude two heads and two pairs of feet, the heads ghastly in their expressions of agony in all its moods, though now and then a face where peace has rested looks out and gives its blessing undismayed.

The feet are pitiful: they that have come so far, and now must go this further, even when all their walks are taken.

To every train that draws up at the right-hand siding there, looking towards the hills, there is added an open truck with a dark-coloured tarpaulin drawn tight down over its top, an iron tank like a big kitchen-sink on wheels. In this have been loaded the fragments that it was not possible to bundle, for bags are scarce, and their cost would make an inroad on the Factory's dividends; and the Factory, though under military organisation, is run at a profit, must so run, or the shareholders will be angry.

For even to this last has Mammon come, and the intellect, that weighs suns in its balance and wants but a fulcrum to lever worlds, divorced from love, ministers in the sty, and, chuckling, counts the hire.

From that truck, last always of the train, a thick dark liquid oozes through invisible joints in its iron frame, and leaves dribblings all along the track. Sometimes the tarpaulin bulges on the top.

When the train draws up – and there is at least one train a day – the wagon doors are unsealed by a stout, fussy official, wearing a skip cap like a station-master's, who clatters along the platforms and bangs down the hasps of the wagon doors one after another, collecting as he passes the little green cards from the frames let into the lower corner of the wagons' sides.

With these cards he fusses off to a small outhouse, where, in an office reeky with disinfectant, divided down the centre by a partition in which is cut an opening like a booking-office window, he bangs them down before a weak-chinned youth who sits at a desk on a high stool, and is off again. The same youth receives a sheaf of papers from the guard of the train, and, adding them to a pile under his hand, resumes his work, entering from the lists to a heavy book before him. Behind him stands a shelf on which a row of similar books lengthens day by day.

Meantime, out upon the platform comes a string of men dressed in overalls and wearing hood-shaped helmets that completely cover their faces and show only two large round eyeholes paned with glass, and a circular nozzle like a telephone receiver stopped by a grating, through which is visible a wad of cotton wool. They carry poles about six feet in length, with an open hook of blunt iron at one end. The overalls are stained with dark patches and drops here and there.

They shuffle at the wagons without words, as if moved by some unholy common instinct rather than by mental impulse, and throw open the doors and commence to rake out the bundles, reaching upward with their long hooks and tugging, then stepping back as the bale thuds its sick impact on the platform.

As they discharge, other figures, dressed in the same ghoulish travesty of monk's vesture, come and go through the sliding doors, now thrown wide. These put out their rakes, hook a bundle by the wire tie and, turning, drag it into the shed, leaning forward as they go, as one drags a sled. The bundles slip easily along the cement paving for it is worn and soon becomes covered with a viscous coating over which the bales slither. A horrible stench fills the air. The men cough dully inside the masks.

Inside the main shed a man steps forward and with a pair of pincers unhooks the wires, letting the bodies sprawl apart on the floor. The place is peopled by a hundred nightmares of decay and dissolution, of inconceivable phantasies of manglement and physical disruption. The stench wells, the steam of its abomination ascends, ascends; no mask can keep it out. No, nor can an iron roof hide it; and One, by whom no violet by the wayside blooms forgotten, whose face is maskless as the day – be assured, O Soul, that He is near.

In this part of the shed is a long corridor, partitioned off from the rest. And at the height of about ten feet from the ground passes an endless chain, propelled by machinery, that clanks ceaselessly onward. Suspended from this chain, at intervals of some three yards, are short lengths of chain terminated by sharp steel hooks that curve their cruel points upward.

A man pushes the bodies forward with a pole under the chain, and another, taking the hook with his right hand and holding the short chain taut with his left, fixes the body by inserting the hook under the breast-bone. The chain clanks and the body goes off, its heels dragging along the floor, the upper portion of the trunk sagging backward, the head rolling, the arms swaying horribly – a sickening travesty of a death-agony.

The chain clanks and another hook hangs, then sags forward with its load. Another hook – another body. The work goes on. The men, poor wights caught in the web of bloodless reason, make an attempt at reverence, which at best can appear but a mockery.

The bodies are dragged up the corridor, and, after passing a corner far up near the end of the shed, ascend into the steaming chamber, where they are detached and, after undergoing a treatment there under the care of another batch of hooded familiars, travel up a belt which, turning at the top, allows them to drop into a huge iron vat, that – heated by a furnace underneath from which comes up a dull roar – simmers like a pot of porridge. In the vat a great macerating-wheel with massive iron cogs revolves slowly, grinding, grinding, half under and half above the surface of that awful stew, its pitiless rim passing six inches from the iron sides of the vat – O Thou, who knowest the end, sustain – and there the bodies, as bodies, cease.

Far underneath in the vat's iron side is a door of iron, tight clamped, and from this, when periodically the vat is emptied, the crushed bones that have sunk to the bottom are drawn out to play their part in the infernal alchemy of Mammon.

64

The exports of the Factory are pig-food, fats, glycerine and manure, brewed and distilled and strained from the mush that once was bodies of men, temples of the – Father, let this cup pass, for I faint. . . .

And to the Tenth Army Section belongs the 85th Regiment; and number 1251 in that regiment is Carl; and along that shuddering via crucis of the railway there, even now, Carl comes.

*   *   *   *   *   *

He woke again to bodily being in a dark and stuffy truck, in which an intolerable odour reigned. He was bound with wires that cut him where they touched, to three other fragments whose souls had passed out in that same agony of battle that had left Carl unconscious, and, by some quirk of that strange house where marvels pass unnoticed, sunk in a marble-still mimicry of death. He was paralysed from crown to toe, rigid in the posture in which he had fallen from the throw of the mine. Nor was speech left to him. Sounds reached him, but he could not answer, nor even groan. Only a little light filters through his eyelids' slit, open so little that they might be closed. And how shall any see the horror in that tiny gleam amid the ghastly tumult of the sheds?

Even as he woke the snorting engine braked at the right-hand platform. The trucks banged in succession upon the hind buffers of the one in front, and he had no more time than to realise his state, and take the odour of the charnel to his waking brain, when the truck door went open with a rasp and a hook was dragging at his chest.

They dumped him on the greasy platform in his bale. The agony of the fall stunned him back to blackness on the threshold of a deeper hell than he had yet known.

*   *   *   *   *   *

When he woke again he did not know at first that black had passed, for he lay uppermost in the bale, his face turned to the sky that spread dark and heavy above him.

Five minutes after he had fallen the knock-off bell had gone. The men that night had been sulky at the order to unload within the last five minutes of a heavy day, and, as their slipshod overseer – already in his Sabbath best – passed through the gate in the engine-cab, gloating over the prospect of his weekly night out in the town six miles away, they had piled their hooks against the shed wall and gone off to the hutches to take off their overalls and eat and afterwards go, too, each to his separate shadow for a time.

The sky is dark. A storm has been gathering all the afternoon and presently closes in, and about eight o'clock rain begins to fall and the wind comes in gusts that grow stronger. The rain-drops patter on the iron roofs of the sheds, faintly at first, then gradually increasing to a steady murmur. For the second time since Carl got his wounds his face is wet from heaven.

And now slowly his numb flesh wakes to feel and move. Silently, mysteriously, the body undoes her magic and lifts the spell laid, perhaps in mercy, on the tattered flesh. He opens his lips, and from his lips come moans and whimpers that the rain's murmur drowns. Presently he slips an arm out of the tie that binds him across the chest, for the bundle has been loosened by that fall from the truck. The ties slacken more as the arm comes out. Then with long moments of stillness, during which agony again swamps him, and struggles stretching across ages of horror, he drags his living body out from its hollow in that bundle of flesh in which decay is already rampant and rises to his feet on the littered platform.

It is a terrible Carl that stands there. He is naked except for a blood-stained rag from his own underclothes, which some relic of decency has ordered should be tied about the corpses' hips. His breast gapes from belly to neck from that bayonet-rip; his left leg hangs crooked, not broken, but shrinking from the ground, every touch of which is a long-drawn woe. His form is blackened by earth and powder fumes, splashed in a dozen places with dark brown blood. He has not eaten for three days. And he is mad.

The rain drives him to shelter, and there in the shed's wall he sees a narrow door. He drags himself along by the wall, and moaning gets to the door – moaning turns the handle. What need of guards and locks here inside that grim fence? He is inside the shed.

A lantern hangs from a hook, just inside, lighted; so, in fact, hangs every night by the whim of some brain sicker or saner than the rest of the shed's servants; and by its yellow glare Carl sees that further horror on the floor. It is ten o'clock.

At twelve he is in a long room, a storehouse of the Factory's ghastly products, lower down the shed, with a door that gives upon the same platform upon which the wagon dumped him. In his hand is the lantern, and his lips gabble unceasingly the words: "All, all, let me see all"; for in Carl's insanity horror reigns – a last vestige of reason – horror at that grisly place in which man's flesh is made to pig's food in a pot; horror at the dangling hooks and those pale rows upon the gratings in the steam-chamber; and fear raised to super-terror, shock by shock, as his reeling brain leaps to knowledge of each new horror.

"Let me see all," he babbles, and from his breast the slow gouts well one by one, for every word a gout, and at every fresh abomination again the words. He has crept up the Corridor of Hooks, followed by his capering shadow, his bare feet slipping in the glush on the floor; he has crouched with outstretched lantern above the Pot; and, down in the cellar, where the iron door opens, has seen the vast heap of splintered bones that feeds the manure-grinders.

And one last horror has been his, one last drop of white hot torture has seared his brain. He came upon it in a cask still unclosed . . . he had been empty for three days . . . and only afterwards he understood. . . .

Now, as he stands there he begins to faint again – he has fainted three times since he took the lantern from its peg – and he staggers, leaning against a heap of a dozen casks piled on the floor against the further wall, some ten yards from the door. His foot knocks away a block, and the casks, piled in three tiers, come down with a rumble, chasing him before them. To him they seem live things, monstrous births of horror, ghouls set there by man to watch and trap him. . . .

A choking moan comes from his throat, and his figure is off down the shed, the lantern dropping from him as he goes. The lantern overturns, the glass shatters, and the spilt oil behind him sputters and runs, blue will-o'-the-wisps flickering upon its pool. Then, as the flame spreads to a litter of stained straw and sawdust that strews one part of the shed floor, a yellow flame springs that with licking fangs reaches and leaps.

But Carl, though he sees the flame's reflection throw his shadow ahead in a giant phantom that capers and sprawls over floor and wall, heeds not, for he hears after him the barrels rumbling, the floor here sloping doorward. And madly he scampers to reach that door before those trundling horrors, bulging forward, should lay their touch upon his heels.

He reaches the door and fumbles at the latch, while out of its corner his frantic eye measures the space between him and the foremost cask and the pace of its roll. He finds the catch, raises it and pulls, and for an instant his heart darts a red pang and his panting brain swims as the door remains fast. Then it gives, and he is out on the platform where those pale figures lie, and the door behind him slams, to shake an instant later with the dull thud of the casks upon its further side.

Instantly his flesh shrinks as the rain impinges on his already shuddering skin and its liquid shell spreads, encasing his body. His torn ear wakes its smart at the bite of the wind; his right leg is a moan that fears the ground and hangs crooked from the knee, twitching, as he rests his weight on the other; his breast, as his blood responds to that urgency of hurry which still shakes him, opens a fresh gape, and from the gash's lower end again a rivulet of red trickles thickly down.

By now the storm has spread its dark forces over all the sky and the moor lies dark beneath great masses of cloud that roll their squadrons over the heavens and deploy and march and counter-march like armies that muster and take positions for attack and charge and withdraw, flirting with lightnings. The rain comes in sudden whirls and gusts, no steady downpour, but like batteries that open suddenly and discharge their wrath and wheel and are gone; and, after a lull, another in turn, choosing its time, bursts its flurry of peltings and shuts and goes dribbling.

There are signs, however, that the night may yet clear, for amid the clouds' jostling battalions now and then a rift shows, and there the black deep of the night sleeps sphered in the moon's light; and here and there a star swims, like a fisher's boat harboured with its light until the storm be past.

As Carl comes out of the door a shower spouts to its height with a roar, shuddering the shed with an echoing downpour on the resounding roof of iron sheeting. A gust of wind whoops round the corner, and, like a troop of phantom vultures, flings itself upon him, whirling round his pale tattered flesh that stands trembling and bewrayed there in that new trial of its discomfort.

But the will is greater than the terrors that assault it, and Carl now shudderingly puts that crane's foot to the ground and is off over the platform to the rails, then down upon the track with a smothered yelp for his leg and then on to the inner fence that lies beyond, limping like a wounded bird, his hand stanching the river at his breast. But where his nest is in all that wild night of storm and agony he does not know – God only knows that. And, oh! it is enough to make a heart crack to see that fragment stagger there, with its backward glance and its totter, flying from man's hard handiwork and flinty heart, hunted like a fox to the moor, and with that pitiful hop of a broken bird. Yet the foxes have their holes, and the birds of the air their nests, but for Carl's head there seems no place of rest. . . .

Now he is at the first fence, and pantingly he drags himself up and puts a leg over, for it is only a few wires high, his whole being a shriek that is smothered in his gaping throat. But when half over a mad fancy whiffs through his sick brain, and, at the sight of those pale figures lying forlorn on the platform yonder, he is back; and over each one he stoops, and patting the poor head, a twisted smile writhing his lips, he says softly: "Sleep, sleepy head, sleep" . . . and at the last one, after he has said this, he pauses, and like a wrestler in his memory he gropes, and then more softly he adds: "Mother will come to you soon" . . . his voice crooning . . . and he is off again with his limp and the load of his torture to the fence.

This time he gets over, not, however, without a fall, at which a boo-hoo of pain conquers and sprawls from his wry mouth. But Carl need not have been afraid then that men would hear him and come as he thought to take him back to that catasta of the sheds behind; for the storm sheltered him, and man's ears are hard, too, like his heart. So only God heard him.

Presently he found the outer fence bar his way, and at that fence his poor heart sank entirely into shadow, for no man unaided might scale it; and he leant against one of the posts of it, bitter, bitter, thinking that now surely was he undone and all his labour at nought.

But in a little he groped in the darkness and reached another post, and then to another he tottered; and, after a long nightmare, in which those posts were commas, he saw the gate and the kennel where the sentry sat.

That night the sentry had drunk well of beer, having gained a wager with a comrade in which the stake was a day's share, and, having taken a turn outside the gate just lately, had come in when the first drops of the shower plashed, and now, huddled in his box, he snored; while the gate, with its lock turned indeed by his fuddled fingers, but clear of its hasp, swung to the wind's breath, showing an inch of space between its iron edge and the post.

So the gate was open; and the guard slept; and Carl passed out.

III
SEPULTURE

THE MOOR took him to its desolation and the winds and waters wrapped him.

Picking his way among the gorse bushes that dotted the moor's face, he went his weary way, his face set towards the forest yonder three miles away; although he knew not whither he went, only that he left the sheds ever farther at his back.

No longer now fearful of a sound, he lets his sick brain say freely her whims and fancies at his mouth, and between his whimpers words come, nonsense for the most part, and echoes from those shelves where the mind stores her records and from which now at random she picks and ponders and drones now a passage and now peevishly is off on a new quest, scattering the dust. . . . And sometimes his head yaws in the wind like a sick ship, and from his slack lips comes a diddle of delirium and a teetering sound of idiocy that gathers its shadows in the house where his soul still lingers.

But soon with his gabble begin to mingle phrases, disjointed at first, but slowly fitting together; with sometimes here and there a ray that breaks and goes or a gleam of peace in which a star swims like a fisher's boat with its light that rides the storm.

Sometimes, too, a sphery thought sails wonderfully athwart that turmoil of raving, a thought too big for the Carl that passed through the anguish of the mount and the horrors of the charnel-house, a glistering orb that sheds calm light upon his suffering soul, like words which they who watch by madmen's beds sometimes hear and wonder at, not understanding but knowing that here no madness speaks.

For a sane man's mind is bounded; and in the pent-house of the brain the soul sets her asylum of sanity and the sanctuary of her self-contemplation that like all else must grow from a little room to big; but a madman's head is a ruined house with walls agape and riven roof through which looms the abyss wherein the planets swing. Not empty are those halls then, nor entirely desolate that Balclutha of the soul; for the soul in her roaming looks in often, visiting the ruined home she loved; and drops sometimes there a flower gathered on the far shores she knows, or whispers there sweet secrets of other whens and wheres; so that those who linger by the door may hear at times, amid the fall of crumbling roof-beams and the flap of swaying shutters, some echo of eternal verities or feel above the odour of rank weeds and rotten grass the subtle perfume of those unknown blooms.

So Carl diddles and droons his way over the moor with that super-sanity of the insane insistently asserting its note, and thus as he goes he murmurs . . . "diddle, diddle, diddle. . . . Oh, that was a cruel rip to give one . . . and struck in anger. But anger is better than hate, for God can be angry, but He would not hate . . . no, not even me . . . diddle, diddle, diddle. And man, sure, has a long way to travel, like me over this moor; and there are storms and blacknesses enough to meet him. But the thing to say is: deeper yet, deeper yet, and still in the end a deeper deep; and in that deep there is a stair starts whose end . . . diddle, diddle, diddle . . . what end is that? . . . Diddle, diddle, diddle, diddle, the cat and the fiddle, the cow . . . yes, the end, oh, that's good now, and Jacob knew it after that long night of his . . . so maybe for me, too, there is a stair at the end of this, maybe even for me too. . . ."

And when later on he stumbled and had a fall, he saw some wild thing run from his scramble, and called to it "pussy, pussy," his mind busy with some memory

77

of firesides; but it did not come, and his tears drizzled from his chin, and he stood saying, "Even the beasts fly from me; and who will take me in then and comfort me?" But his home, had he known it, was not far then nor was his comforter unmindful.

Then, seeing the moon through a rift of the storm – which by now was beginning to break up and clear – cruising like a swan in her pool of gloom, he said: "There you go, there you go, you child bereft and far from home; well may you muse upon this cruising human-home, for she is heavy laden . . . and a tear might well fall some night from you; for her freight of care and heartache is past all cargo-mark, Father, Thou knowest" . . . and again a spasm shook him at that "Father", and he diddled.

And further on he stumbled over a spade with a broken handle that some workman had left lying there at the time those sheds were built; and, listlessly, after gazing on it for some time, he took it up and carried it with him, murmuring: "Here is a spade, Carl; and here is Carl, spade; but whether Carl has found the spade, or the spade Carl, neither of them knows; for this spade has a broken handle and is thrown out on the moor; and I, too, am broken-handled, and thrown out too, so that I am thought useless by all men, save it be to dig my own grave . . . diddle, diddle. . . . So we may as well go together, spade, for none will have us, not even God; for if I be without a handle, how may He take me up?". . . and his foot caught in a stone and he fell upon his face.

As he lay, he lost his spade and groped, and for a moment had a pang of loneliness at the loss of it, but presently found it a little way from him as he lay, and felt immediately better of that pang and followed his musing vacantly, his lips moving as of their own will.

"But it seems I was wrong now, for here is nothing but a broken spade; but when I lost it I was forlorn, and finding it was happy again; so that even a broken spade is some use it seems, if one love it. And even when it is utterly broken up and mouldered I suppose it is not utterly destroyed, for that I am sure of, but its substance must pass into other spades, or into other and finer tools. But look now; someone planned the spade before it was made, and took iron and wood and put his plan in them and clothed his plan in spade; but the plan was in the mind, and a man's thoughts now do not rot. A thought is not a thing, and man can't get at it to rot it or to break it. So you see, Carl, the spade is good and need not be afraid" . . . and at that he rose again, and as he went hopping

79

on amid the gorse his brows wrinkled and his eye puzzled, as with a great thought that would not be tamed to speech.

Once as he went he saw suddenly a dark form stretch out before him on the ground like a great evil thing that lay in wait to betray his feet, and he started, all his fear swift-turned on him and his heart sinking, for that menace was sudden, and awful seemed that form; yet saying "What cannot harm spade surely cannot harm me," he made a step and found that it was his shadow, cast by a glare that had waked behind him on the moor.

That thought with which he wrestled was very near then and his soul was a Bethesda pool which it seemed an angel's wings almost stirred, but at the light he turned, thinking day came then; and again the pool waited.

Day was not yet, and it was an evil light that he saw far away whence he had come. The lantern he had dropped in his flight down the shed had set its flame's contagion firm in that sinful house, before any of its minions had waked to its menace in that wild and roaring night, and now the conflagration was well under way, lighting up the moor with the glare of its destruction.

Great billows of smoke, heavy and greasy as with the evil that had dwelt there, rolled far away towards the river before the wind that had now died to a breeze, and tongues of deep orange flame shot up, from which sparks whirled upwards. Now and then great flots of fire, detached, soared a moment, and flickered and went out.

The rain had ceased, the sky was clearing and the murmur of the flame came out to Carl dimly, he being now about two miles away from the sheds and about a mile from the road yonder.

He stood in an irregular circle of gorse bushes and watched that far outroar of red fury growing and the sparks and flame-flots fly their brief flight and go. . . . "As the sparks fly . . ." he murmured. Then suddenly he was aware that even here the glare reached, showing him dimly, and, still faithless in man's hard heart and the hand that seemed always against him, he sank, thinking he would surely be discovered; "and goodness knows," he thought, "what new thing they will do to me if that happens."

After a little he looked out and saw the fire grow and black figures run about the foot of the furnace; and presently, darkling, with a grim resolve in his eye, he took the spade and began to dig. And as he dug in the face of the moor, he spoke to himself: "If I stay here I am caught by those devils yonder, and go further I cannot, God knows; for here I am foundered at the last and my life must be saved or spent in this spot, for I am not a bird though I hop like one" ... and a twisted smile broke on his lips to a sob, he being then truly near his end and his flesh but a living wince in which the soul lingered. And now as he dug he sobbed: "God, God – if you do see and it is not an untruth – look, I have borne my part, surely; nevertheless, what more of my share may be to come I'll bear – I'll bear. ... But a man is not a camel, now ... not a camel ... and it is time to make an end. Here, then, I will dig my grave, and I will be buried in the earth; for in her is sweetness and good rest and comfort ... " and he went on digging with his broken spade.

Presently, after half an hour's labour, crouching there, during which his breast gaped again and drops of blood fell on the spadeful he turned, he had carved a shallow ditch the length of a man, two feet across and about a foot and a half deep, but then could do no more, feeling death near; and he said: "I will lay me down in this grave that I have made and here will I compose myself to sleep, for my limbs are aweary, aweary, and my heart heavy laden; and to no further bourne came all the tribes of earth, no, and to no better rest, for truly man is dust, and darkness the portion of his days."

But before he lay down in the grave he had another memory, and he knelt there in his pain and nakedness to pray. And when he had knelt to pray he would have said the Lord's Prayer, for that seemed to him a good prayer; but he found he had forgotten it, and he could only sob . . . and after a little he said "Mother . . . mother" . . . and that comforted him, for God had made him as a little child again.

He took the spade and lay in the grave, and, closing his eyes, he said softly: "This surely is the end of my pain and I can die and be at rest for ever" . . . and after a little . . . "But if there is a God He will raise me." And he slept.

IV

RESURRECTION

I N A SWIFT, easy-rolling car that night two men
sped along a road, leaving ever farther behind them
the snake-line where the Beast raged and in which Hill
50 was a boil of torment.

Before and behind the car went two others, each
keeping its distance from the middle car and each with
four soldiers on board.

Of the two men in the car, one was a burly figure
dressed in a Marshal's uniform under a grey cloak. His
face was massive and heavy-jowled, a grim face with
an eye to be feared, for pity was not in it.

The other was a slighter man, whose face was almost totally hidden by the turned-up collar of his coat,
above which, in the shadow of his helmet, his eyes
gleamed with an insolent stare. His loose cloak, thrown
open, showed a glitter here and there on the uniform
beneath, for they had been to a review of raw troops,
these two, where for once in a while such gewgaws had
their use to gild the bitter pill of death.

Silence hung in the car between those two and with gloomy looks their eyes roved through the windows as they sped through the countryside, deserted and still in the slowly-waking grey of a storm-washed dawn, it being now about four in the morning.

The rain of the night had ceased to fall and the skies were clearing, the clouds rolling away horizonwards in a jostling tumult of murky billows; and a fresh wind blew, with a promise in it of a glorious day to be. The wheels of the car splashed now and then through pools of rain water.

The figures in the car sat motionless, each communing with his mind's images and getting little comfort there, it might be seen. The man with the shadowed face broke the silence. "So they fight," he said.

The other man turned on him a dour look, something between respect and contempt. "So," he said, "they fight. But what can they do? A handful!" He flicked his coat sleeve. He was still for a space, then spoke again, his dour smile twitching his face. "War broods," he said, "and all her eggs are not hatched yet."

The slight man looked at him sideways. "Nor laid," he said between closed teeth and laughed loudly at his own wit.

The car at that moment swerved round a bend of the road, which followed here the line of a forest's edge. In front and on one side of the car they saw a wide expanse of moor bounded by a distant ridge of hills.

A mist lay over the face of the low land, a mist that rose like an evil thing born of quags and marshes, that hurried to be gone before the dawn. And far out on the moor a great red eye glared, a dark crimson pupil in an iris of orange light that hung spectral-like above the wold and pulsed and ogled like an unholy eye.

The smaller man leant forward and looked intently at that far-away conflagration swimming in the mist. For a full ten seconds he regarded it and, as he looked there into that red pupil, his eyes in the shadow of his helmet threw back a glint of red, for even at that distance a faint tinge of its fury dyed the air like the glare from a furnace door, flushing the wall of trees on the further side of the car. One would have thought that the fire fascinated him, for as he looked his head went slowly forward as a bird goes to a snake. His lips went down at the corners and he laughed harshly.

"Look!" he said, nudging the other; "someone is warming himself this morning. What place can that be?"

The other pondered a moment; then, reading easily from the map of his well-stored, well-ordered super-mind, he answered: "This is where the Utilisation Factory of the Tenth Army Section is situated, and those should be the buildings that are ablaze yonder. The flame spreads from below upwards," he added with a laugh. "The main building is a big one, and there should be a crash soon; it should be worth watching. I suppose it came from above," and he glanced upward; "but I thought they were safe here. Curse those planes!" Thus with idiot lips he, too, gabbled the high truths given him.

The other was about to lie back on the cushions, his mind ready to rove from that new toy of the fire, when a whim seized him, given as he was to fantastic tricks. He leaned forward and rapped the front window, and the car drew up. The cars ahead and behind also stopped, and by the time he was on the road a group of officers stood around him at a respectful distance.

"Come, Marshal," he said, "we will walk a little way in this fresh air and see that nearer. The crash would not be complete without us," and he chuckled.

The other in the car got up lumberingly, and with a "You command, Highness," which scarcely disguised his grumpiness, stepped out beside him on the moor. Four of the others fell in behind, some ten yards off, walking stiffly, their eyes straight ahead and unmindful of the moor's beauties, for even in its evil it was a thing of loveliness there in the presage of the dawn.

The sky was now almost completely clear and the mist was paling rapidly, waning the anger of that red eye that glowed before them. Behind them the dark fringe of the forest was faintly tinged with rose against the night that rolled back yonder in the west. Far off, the hills lay on the horizon, and in the sky above the hills the Morning Star hung clear as a spark of crystal light.

The flame that drew them burned ahead and they trudged forward, their feet making a sound of chugging in the quaggy patches that interspersed the firmer ground.

They had come the better part of a mile from the road when the smaller of those two figures ahead started and gripped the other by the arm. "Look!" he said. They stopped. The four figures behind halted.

They had come to the edge of an irregular circle of gorse bushes, enclosing a patch of firmer ground. In the centre of the little arena thus formed was visible a heap of newly turned earth. By the side of the mound was a shallow grave, and in the grave lay a naked man with a great wound in his breast and a broken spade by his side. Upon the air came a sound of moaning.

The bulky figure of the Marshal moved a pace in front of the other, then, stayed by something more than the strange terror of that figure lying there, he stopped, and his voice came in a gruff whisper. "Some madman," he said. "He must be one of the men from the sheds. Come back, Highness. I will have him covered and dispatched somewhere."

On the verge of his answer the other gripped the Marshal's arm again and pointed. . . .

The body of Carl had been lying in the grave with his head towards the two who had come thus upon him and, as the smaller man raised his hand, pointing at him, he rose till he was sitting in the hollow, his back still towards them, so that he did not see them with his eyes.

He rose sitting, and before him, as those eyes now opened, he saw the hills, and above them that Star hanging like a spark of crystal in the sky.

He looked, and slowly his moans died away. Wonder stirred behind the tiredness in those eyes then and slowly broke, flowering like the blossom of a babe's calm glance when first its eyelids open beneath its mother's kiss. The twitchings smoothed away from that racked flesh, as if a touch had healed the scars of all his woe. Then slowly, with a motion of infinite yearning, he raised his arms, stretching them wide towards the hills and the beacon that hung above them.

His voice came, and his voice was calm and deep, and "Oh, there's a music there," he said, with a movement of his head, first from side to side, then bowing. ... "Oh, there's a music there ... that beats the bleat of all man's music; ... and a light ... a light ... that's not a candle."

And in Carl's heart then truly there was music – and a psalm unheard of man; for he had come through that valley whose shadow is Death, and lifted up his eyes unto the hills; and a presence stood with him in his house and used his lips for ends beyond his ken.

The watchers there stood motionless, watching him, hearing those words dimly, yet clear in the morning-still.

And he went on: "Again, again my cup is prepared, and behold I take it gladly. Father, let it not pass from me; for though the labour is heavy, the labourer is strong." He stood up. "I come, and the morning comes with me," said his voice, rising with a note of anthems. "Behold the earth, O Son, the vineyard where the ripe grape hangs her clusters of full-blooded fruit, ripe for yet another vintage, another of the luscious harvest-homes of God. And though my feet be heavy on both grape and the stalk, though the lees must be cast out until another pressing, Thy wine-bin shall be love in the end to overflowing, and not one drop remain ungathered."

He turned and looked on those two, his eyes placid, yet with a gaze in them under which they stirred uneasily.

He smiled slowly, not a fear there, nor a doubt. . . . "What seek ye?" he said. "For if ye seek this Carl whom ye numbered with a tag, stamped upon one side with a crown and the number eighty and five, and upon the other with the number one thousand two hundred and fifty and one, he is with me, but ye cannot touch him; for I hold him now, and presently Another. And if ye seek me who am with him in his house, me indeed ye may touch if ye will, but the will is not in ye. Yet love a moment as this one came at last to love, and ye shall sup with me at my table."

The Marshal strode forward, his burly figure looming grossly by that worn flesh there in the grave. "Who are you and what are you doing here, fellow?" he said with a surprised and angry eye, his large well-ordered mind fretful at this jarring figure, this thing not in that mind's reckoning, thrust thus suddenly into its ken.

He paused, and from Carl no answer came, but he looked at those two with a clear eye, not surprised he but calm as summer-sky. The Marshal took a pace. "Salute your Emperor," he said.

The voice of Carl spoke softly and he turned upon that burly form his cool pupil. "My Emperor truly I do salute," he said; "and bow myself wholly down before him; but not this emperor, but another whom you know not now with the mind; but the soul there in her secret chambers knows Him and makes her obeisance to Him in that hall where from of old He has set His holy throne." He paused.

The Marshal's dull eye grew dark, and again he spoke, saying gruffly: "Do you not know who we are?"

And Carl's voice answered: "Yes, I know you truly, you and the other there, but not as ye know yourselves, but in another glass than the eye scans. You are begotten of the Oneness, that yet is not the One, of its separation into its elements in order that meeting they may apprehend and mate in conscious union. And yours is the grosser part, and a hard man you are, with adamant in your heart now; but He who fused the adamant, He

93

will fuse you too, never fear; and soon in His chosen vessels with the fire out of the mouth of a babe you will be blasted; and if the torture of the fire has been long, yours will be as the slag and lava till you learn, and do, His will. . . . Long has the earth waited, but now the hour is at hand. Even now my feet are wonder on the hills; my voice gathers in the blast; the brush of my wings shakes the bastions of the darkness. . . . I come, the Chosen of God, the Cosmic, planet-chapleted and unashamed, anointed with the chrism of blood that is the Jordan-water preferred before the rivers of Pharpar and Abana. . . . Woe unto ye, the hard; he through whose lips I speak is sifted, but ye are still to sift. Yet a little while and I will kiss him, but ye I will spew out of my mouth . . . before my breath ye shall be as the thistle's beard in the whirlwind, as snow-drifts at the thaw. . . . Not that ye shall be cast away for ever, but that first I will eat the ripe, but the green not yet."

His voice was a trumpet – in his eye the lightning like an eagle homed. For a moment a ray from the waning fire lit a streamer of mist that seemed to flame from his right hand outwards like a sword . . . then passed, and he smiled again.

He stood up, drawing himself taut from the toes, reaching . . . his arms outstretched . . . a tatter of rag still swathed about his hips . . . on his breast the red gash agape. They saw him a pale figure against the murk . . . strangely reminiscent . . . he was lifted up . . . light beat from his face . . . Morning Star was at his brow . . . the grave under his feet.

For a moment the two before him tensed. In the stillness their breathing was heard with a hissing intake.

Then the body's arms came slowly down and the voice from the lips of Carl broke like a chant upon the morning air; now crooning as a mother's voice above the downy babe's head nested in her breast; now with the note with which in the valley of the shadow a man yearns back through the years for those breasts of peace again; or whispering like a lover's insistent whisper at his beloved's ear; or, again, rolling deep-chested as the anthem of a priest inspired:

"*Sing unto the Lord, O Earth; and all ye stars give answer. Praise Him, ye heavens that He has made, with all your chanting choirs. For from His love He made you, and cannot leave you; all you in Him, no speck in you not held within His hand.*

"*And though He let you stray like babes, yet a road He gives you and a gate; and though you wander far from His father-hand, in the end He leads you right;*

and will bring you back into His heart's harbour and holy home of Love.

"In His House He has decked a bridal chamber and there He waits you as a bride the bridegroom, with the spousal kiss ripe upon his lips, sweet, sweet; and the lamps lighted about the couch and the curtains drawn.

"Sing unto the Lord, O Earth; and all ye stars give answer. Praise Him, ye heavens that He has made, with all your chanting choirs."

He ceased; then bowed his head. Then again he looked at them with that eye of summer-calm. "What seek ye?" he said.

The gruff voice of the Marshal seemed to falter a moment on his lips, but with a wrench he spoke. "Who are you?" he asked again.

"I am the King of the World," the lips of Carl answered, and his voice was like a challenge. Then with a softer tone he went on: "If I am come here and declare it unto you, it is not for you alone, nor for him only that is present in this house with me, but that the purposes of Him that sent me may be fulfilled. For out of the Father comes the Son, which is the Father also, and must be first in Him. So also is that earthly birth that now must be. But the father here begets not the son in spirit; but through him only in this case may the

Spirit of the Son pass. For this one was tried in the fire and refined, and was a worthy vessel in the end; in his heart holiness and loving-kindness and a child-like faith in the most high ways of God. And if the vessel were tainted a strong spirit would yet take away a cloud with it; and it is needful that this be as crystal, or the labour would be in vain."

He groaned, and on his brow, though no ruffle showed, the sweat stood. "I speak riddles to you, but before we leave this spot, all this and more shall be accomplished. And now – I go." He ceased, and made a step . . . looking at the two as though expectant.

The two cloaked figures in front of him did not stir from their places, but the bulkier made a movement of his hand as if he would have summoned the four that stood together some yards behind.

The other man put out his hand and stayed the gesture. "Let him be," he said; "the men from the sheds will find him, and in any case we cannot be troubled with him. He hasn't got long, poor fellow."

The Marshal shrugged. "You command," he said. "Shall we go?" He half turned.

The pale figure stopped a moment, and they could hear a murmur from it as though a voice spoke with itself there. Then the voice of Carl was raised.

"Look!" he said. "I go to preach to the people, to stir them so that soon they will come and take your crown away and break it, and make a better crown for an Emperor mightier than you. The Beast you serve draws near his end. Think you that it was written in vain: 'Out of the eater shall come forth meat and out of the strong sweetness?' You have made yourselves his priests, but there is a murmur that grows, even now a fama-clamosa is set against you that you must answer." He made another step.

"The Slayer of the Beast is afoot," his voice pealed. "I have eaten of his food yonder in the sty that burns, and am his master even in the flesh. I have taken the measure of your works and weighed them and found them wanting – and the Carl ye numbered with a tag has set alight your sinful house." He pointed to the smouldering sheds. "Your empire and its abomination" ... He fixed upon the smaller man a look of judgment ... "is even now in spirit at an end." Again the mist lit from his right hand. "And I go to stir the people." He made another step.

The slighter figure in front of him turned and spoke to the other. "Have him sent to a madhouse," he said.

But the other brooded with a heavy brow, looking at Carl. He swept his hand across his brow, puzzling, as one tries to brush the cobwebs from some far memory.

"I have heard that tone before," he said, "but where I forget; which for me is strange. But to let him go, Highness, were madness as great as his. This voice makes converts, and even now there is a murmur among the people which grows. . . . He has seen too much, I think, and by his own words he fired the Factory yonder. In any case he is a rag already. Since he has made his bed let him lie in it and save a firing party."

The slight man turned away with a "Well, well, do what you think best, Marshal, but quickly; I wash my hands of it," and stood, back to those two, his cloak aflap in the gentle wind that now stirred, his figure grey there in the whispering dawn. The other fumbled a moment beneath his cloak, then as that white figure went stepping, all its limp forgot, he made a swift stride – was beside it. His hand went up with a glint of blue steel, and a sharp crack barked in the stillness, sending a startled bird skyward from a nearby bush. Carl staggered a few steps backward, and as his backward step went over the edge of the grave, he fell, and lay there upon his back, his length along the length of the shallow pit.

While a breath might come and go they remained there, these three, together in the flesh after so many years. . . .

The mists of the dawn were rising all about them on the moor, and at that moment the cold grey of the breaking light seemed shadowed, dimming the angry smoulder from the far-off sheds, where the fire by now died, and the motionless figures of the other four that stood grouped some yards apart. Then over the hills came the dawn, a tiny rim of red at first that grew as the eye watched it – and suddenly all the mist was glorious with tints of mother-of-pearl and opal and rose.

The Marshal slipped the thing he held in his hand under his cloak and turned, but the other, with a lift of the eyebrows and a sidelong glance, showed him a twitch that quivered and passed and quivered in the flesh that lay in the ditch, and he turned again and took a pace and looked down.

Then he stepped down with a heavy tread upon the body that lay there in the grave, and setting his foot upon the neck, pressed with a jerk of his full weight until the tautened sinews dragged the chin down to dent the upper of his boot-toe. There was a dull snap.

And never again moved Carl; for there beneath that heel his story closed, and, before the snap of his atlas passed, his soul was where no heel could harm him. And though no soul-bell sped nor priest shrove him, though to the outward eye his house was utterly destroyed, him also the mansion of the Father gathered.

* * * * * *

And at that hour, in her garret in a far town, Ann, the wife of Carl, laid suddenly down her sewing and put her hand to her side, feeling a pang there; then to the bed she tottered with a moan and lay where never more Carl's weight would press, her soul all a trouble-ment of new darkness and new light. For between two that God makes three there is a bond, God knows, that man knows not.

And, going back, those two sat silent in their car; and between them an echo of words hung heavy, and long shadows of thoughts swept now and then through those chambers where each man dwells with the images he has made and which one by one he must break before he finds himself and knows the Maker from the Made. Yet what those shadows brought them, whether their hearts were touched with pity or whether they brushed them aside as idle fancies, they only know, each of them – they, and God who knows all things.

But this only is here written, that after a long spell of that grim silence between them in the car, he of the shadowed face said to the other: "By the way, Marshal, do you remember that regiment and number?" And the other with the big, well-stored, well-ordered mind said: "Yes, I have made a note of them." Then at the end of a further silence the first one said: "Oh, well, if he had a wife, see that she gets the cross – he did his bit anyway." So Carl's bit is done, and a note is duly made; and the car rolls on.

A week later a flat package, stamped with many seals, was put into Ann's hands, and when she had tremblingly undone the tapes and shattered the crimson wax that fell in flakes, be-dabbling dreadfully the floor, she found a box, and inside the box a cross.

In this way the cross of Carl came home to his wife, Ann; and the cross of Carl that so terribly he earned is now Ann's, and she bears it.

But for his slayers also is a cross prepared; and that cross is more terrible than Carl's. For as the deep is, so also is the steep.

*When the flow of these waters was over,
a voice said: The work of the spirit is
done; what remains is a labour of the
mind.*

*The vessel gives it not as it was
given, but as in a figure of things spiritual, and through a dark glass.*

*But Another comes to tell it clear
and sweet; and a blind man shall see
Him, and at His voice the ears of the
deaf rejoice.*

Peace be with you.

July 1917

A BIOGRAPHICAL NOTE

Poet, Anonymity to Acclaim and Back
by Andrew Graham-Yooll

WALTER OWEN (1884–1953), poet, mystic and merchant, a Scot, may not be forgotten, but almost. He deserves more. He was, after all, the first translator of the *Martín Fierro* into English, published in London and New York in 1935, though he should also be remembered for his own classical poetry and novels. We all have something worth remembering.

You can Google Owen and reach *A Guide to Supernatural Fiction*. But there's not much more. The best and relatively recent writing to be found on Owen is an article by the Scottish academic, John Walker, in the *Buenos Aires Herald* (6 August 1977) and, more extensive, there is an essay also by Walker, in one of those learned journals that nobody reads, the *Latin American Literary Review* (vol. III no. 5, 1974). It is about Owen and the art of translation of poetry, an excellent portrait of the man, his work and his literary theories. The biography written by the late Baroness

Charlotte de Hartingh, *Servitor on an Outer Plane*, published by the Instituto Cultural Walter Owen in Buenos Aires in 1966, is hard to find.

Walter Hubbard Owen was born July 14, 1884, in Glasgow, of a Scottish mother and a father of Welsh ancestry. Owen as a teenager trained in shipping in Glasgow, and in Buenos Aires business circles would be best known as a customs clearance expert. Owen lived in Buenos Aires and latterly Martínez for most of his life; his most distant forays, apart from three visits to England and France, were to Tigre, where he rowed in the company of a faithful band of friends. His published literary works include four volumes of poetry (under the *nom de plume* of *Gauthier de St Ouen*, a "Frenchification" of Owen): *Amor Viri* (1912), 50 sonnets; *Aurora* (1913), which included *The Cosmic Song* (1910), one poem dedicated to ill-fated air pioneer, Jorge Newbery, who was one of his good friends; *Sonnets to Soldiers and Other Verses* (1918); *The Sonnets of G.S.O.*, published in the thirties. But his greatest work, for which he is remembered, if at all, were the eight book-length translations of epic poems and history from Spanish classics.

These he called his "transvernacularisations" (he refused to call them translations). Published in a limited edition by Blackwell's in Britain in 1935, and immediately after in a full commercial printing in the US, the *Martín Fierro* by José Hernández (1834–1886), is his best known and celebrated publication. This he followed with *Fausto* (1886) by Estanislao del Campo (1834–1880) in 1943, which is described as weak by comparison with *Fierro*. Then came *Don Juan Tenorio* (1844) by Spaniard José Zorrilla y Moral (1817–1893); the Chilean epic *La Araucana* by Spaniard Alonso de Ercilla y Zúñiga (1533–1594) and the Uruguayan national poem *Tabaré*, also in 1934, by Juan Zorrilla de San Martín (1855–1931), published by Unesco, in 1956; the historical poem by Martín del Barco Centenera (1535–1602), *"La Argentina" and the Conquest of the River Plate* (1602), published post mortem in 1965 by the Instituto Cultural Walter Owen, edited by Patrick Dudgeon; next came the Chilean classic *Arauco Domado* by Pedro de Oña (1570–1643), which he completed in his hospital bed five weeks before his death; and *Narrative of the Expedition of Sir Francis Drake* by Juan de Castellanos (1522–1607), published for the first time in Spanish in 1921. (Apologies for the accumulation of dates but they do give an idea of the remarkable volume of the man's work.)

The last three "transvernacularisations" were produced from his bed at the British Hospital, which he entered on 13 December 1949, never to leave until his death. The last two books were not published. But all his work referred back to his first, *Martín Fierro*. Of this work, he wrote, "A translation, especially of verse, in order to have any value as literature, should read like an original work. Clarity and ease are essential and they are worth purchasing at the price of a certain degree of verbal accuracy ... A false note, a too unfamiliar image, a forced simile, the translation of a dead metaphor into a live one ... a reference that is plain and immediately comprehensible in the original [but] is too obscure in the translation for the reader to grasp, any or all of these may be the result of a too faithful adherence to the text". (John Walker, *Latin American Literary Review*)

For his "transvernacularisation" of the *Martín Fierro*, Owen developed a certain ceremony. For a time he took rooms in the hotel off Plaza de Mayo where José Hernández was said to have written part of his epic (and he also took rooms at Bolivar 609, where the author of *Tabaré* had resided for a time). The *Martín Fierro* required a degree of ceremony which would remain with Owen for years. He built a rustic wooden desk and chair at which to work, he put aside his daytime office garb and donned a monk's robe, and wrote by candle light with a quill pen, watched over by his cat, Dusky, who was ever-present on the work table and in the writing, with shopping reminders in the margins such as, "liver for Dusky, Players 2 pkts (cigarettes), Pinot white", etc. There are quite a few references to the Players and the Pinot. Dusky died on May 20, 1933, the day after the translation was completed, an incident which had Owen searching for its mystical meaning. The poet's hard slog is recorded in a "*laborómetro*" that details the daily progress of translation. His notes describe his style in translation; some of his lines should be guidelines for present-day translators. ". . . I have tried to present to English readers a version of [an epic] that reads like an original English poem, flavoured with the idiom and diction of the times, and free from the stilted style and un-English air that often makes translations of foreign poems irksome to minds appreciative of the beauties of our mother tongue. It is obvious that if this object is to be attained, textual fidelity must be subordinated to ease, clarity, rhythm, harmony, tone, and the other elements of style. We are interposing our own consciousness between the conceptual and the linguistic centres [. . .] and rewriting his poem as he would have written it if he had spoken English . . . " (*Servitor* . . . , page 186)

For weeks after publication of *Martín Fierro* in English, Owen was a kind of folk hero in Buenos Aires. People would track him down at lunch in his regular restaurants and ask him for autographs in their copies of the book. Failing that, he had to sign scraps of paper and even napkins.

All of Owen's original writings and translations were aimed at helping to build "a bridge to better understanding between the peoples" of the world, an objective which he repeatedly used in descriptions given to one of his principal mentors, the former British ambassador, Sir Eugen Millington-Drake (1889–1972), well known in Buenos Aires for his lectures on the Battle of the River Plate in 1939 and in Montevideo for helping to fund out of pocket the start of the Pluna airline), and friends, including Courtenay Luck, one of the best known mystics in the British community in Buenos Aires, and brothers Luis and Juan Alejandro de Marval, among others. Millington-Drake described the *Martín Fierro* translation as having "the raciness of an old Border ballad."

Owen wrote one philosophical/historical treatise, *The Ordeal of Christendom* (Grant Richards,

1938), wherein he argues that "Christ is the only evolutionary factor in consciousness", and two novels. His reputation as an author of supernatural fiction rests with these two novels.

Of these his most important fiction was, again, his first book *The Cross of Carl* (published by Grant Richards, London, in 1931), written at one sitting in an evening in 1917 – this after his first extended hospitalisation for a painful abdominal complaint. It was accepted for publication in Britain the following year, but was stopped by the censor. It was seen as brutal, surrealistic and bleakly anti-war, too harsh for the immediate period following the Great War. It was finally published in London in 1931, and in the US by Little, Brown and Company (Boston), also in 1931. It was described as a rhythmic fantasy in prose.

The "Carl" of the title is a foot soldier in the trenches of World War I. Mistaken for dead he is bundled off to a rendering plant for what we might now term recycling. *The Cross of Carl* was originally inspired by an element of anti-German newspaper propaganda and an alleged bilocation of personality brought upon the author through dosages of opium, though also influenced by his strong mystic beliefs. Owen's biographer, Charlotte de Hartingh, says he, "took an intense interest in the stimulative effect that drugs effected over the creative faculties." Rather cautiously, she says that, "He was by no means the first man of letters, nor the last, to be fascinated by those results ... [he] has left a detailed description of his impressions while under the sway of opium ..." Carl's nationality is never made wholly clear (though German is usually inferred, based upon source materials and several late-chapter hints). Thus the Cross of the title can be alternately read to mean the Iron Cross, the Victoria Cross, or both. The *Times Literary Supplement* review, on 16 July 1931, called the book "A war allegory" that "brings back the ugly side of war psychology; it is a description of one of the 'corpse factories' of legend – an unbearably ghastly description. 'Sepulture' is a description of how the dying Carl digs his own grave. 'Resurrection' ends the allegory on a note of mystical triumph. This record of what the author himself describes as 'an abnormal pathological process' induced by the psychic perturbations of the War, is put forward in the belief that the experience may foreshadow some sort of development in the collective consciousness of mankind." It was foresight, in a way, but of something more horrible, which would be the Nazi holocaust of World War II.

His other fiction, *More Things in Heaven*, published by Andrew Dakers (London, 1947), has a narrator (Owen) and a mystic adept named Merlin Alaska investigate a case of Spontaneous Human Combustion. The trail of clues, found in ancient documents, manuscripts and travelogues, leads to the discovery of a two-thousand-year-old Zoroastrian curse upon the descendants of Alexander the Great. Really very modern stuff, if you pick up Umberto Eco's *In the Name of the Rose*.

Many of his poems, articles, and stories remain uncollected, having been published mainly in *The Standard* newspaper and some rare magazines and self-printed pamphlets. These were always signed G.S.O., or the full pen name, "lest he fall into disgrace in Buenos Aires business circles through writing poetry!" (*Servitor*, p. 95) In blunt terms, the business community saw poetry as something for "pansies" in the jargon of that time. Owen was known publicly as a scrupulous, punctilious, member of the staff of Messrs. Bessler, Waechter & Co. Ltd., import agents, and after fifteen years, as manager and model businessman at Juan McCall & Co., customs clearing agents, where he moved in 1928. In his carefully managed spare time Owen was also a bibliophile, his biographer describes him as a mystic, and others see him as a Baconian (follower of Sir Francis Bacon – proponent of the methodical observation of facts, also said by some to have been the real author of Shakespeare's writings), a Grand Master in the small Beacon Lodge Theosophist and Philosophical Society, and Duke of the Island of Redonda in the Caribbean Sea, a fictitious court created by a novelist of his acquaintance with a base on a remote rock. He also enjoyed sports, rowing for the Tigre Boat Club and was the founder of a boxing club.

Though a pacifist of sorts he attempted to enlist for service on the British side during both World Wars. But he was blind in one eye lost in a childhood accident in 1895, aged 11, while playing with a home chemical set with his brother Tom. In spite of this severe disability, he would later volunteer repeatedly for the two European wars, and was obviously rejected each time. His next blow was the death of his mother, Ellen, a teacher, who had nursed him through the recovery of sight in the remaining eye; she died suddenly. His father, a shipping agent, who in 1889 had brought the family to Montevideo, first, thence Buenos Aires, decided to send his youngest son to live with two aunts in Glasgow, there for his secondary studies at Hillhead High School. On leaving school he worked for a chemical company and later a shipping agent, which paved the way to stowing on a ship that took him back to Buenos Aires. He was eighteen when he began life in earnest in Argentina in June 1902. He seems to have returned to the United Kingdom, and once to France, on three quite secret visits, in 1920, 1924 and 1928, on one occasion to meet his girlfriend Beryl and her daughter, at school in southern France. One of those visits was in pursuit of the leading mystic of the time in Europe, Georges Ivanovich Gurdjieff (1877–1949).

His love life was not what you might call a success. After early failure of an intense love with a woman only named as "Sylvia", apparently due to parental disapproval (she visited him briefly on his deathbed at the British Hospital), Owen was married on the rebound to Lily Edith Turner, daughter of a Central Argentine Railway officer. The marriage on June 6, 1914, two months before the outbreak of war, was doomed from the start: they were totally different characters. She was a lively person intent on a busy social life, he a subdued, reclusive and solitary individual. They were together for only a few weeks. Separation was followed by attempted reconciliations and failed reunions amid regular arguments. Owen provided for Edith financially all his life, but in 1917, aged 33, he met a woman named Beryl who became the partner he sought. He said he had found happiness with her. They would be together up to her death in 1947. He became severely depressed.

His final years, ill and unable to work, seemed to have been filled with projects. Sometimes he lay in bed on his side, dictating translations and correspondence to a secretary, Diana de Marval, the daughter of his friend. He lived on his savings and the help of friends, and of his brother Tom, whom he would ask to sell off his valuable first editions, kept at his last home in Martínez, to pay for expenses.

He died on September 24, 1953, in hospital, his ashes buried at the British cemetery in Chacarita, where a commemorative plaque was placed. A bust by the Uruguayan sculptor José Luis Zorrilla de San Martín (1891–1975), son of the author of *Tabaré*, is in the Hillhead High School library, and in Buenos Aires there is one by José Fioravanti (1896–1977).

May 2012

The Bulletin Argentine, British Community Council, vol. LV, no. 1

http://depoetaspoesia.blogspot.com/2012/05/walter-owen.html

Special thanks to Doreen Dalrymple, manager at Hillhead High School, Glasgow, for finding many documents relative to the life of Walter Owen. With thanks to the director of the Güiraldes Museum, at San Antonio de Areco, Mrs Cynthia Smyth, and to her staff, Mariana Rios, Bibiana Bovetti, Patricia Lucero, Valeria Urruchúa, y Marcela Cigarelli. The originals of Owen's Martín Fierro *in English are held at the Museum.*